A LITTLE IN LOVE A LOT

Poems by

PAUL HOSTOVSKY

Main Street Rag Publishing Company
Charlotte, North Carolina

Library of Congress Control Number: 2011923733

ISBN: 978-1-59948-303-0

Produced in the United States of America

Main Street Rag
PO Box 690100
Charlotte, NC 28227
www.MainStreetRag.com

ACKNOWLEDGEMENTS

Thanks to the following publications in which many of these poems, or earlier versions of them, previously appeared:

Alimentum, Amoskeag, Asinine, Aunt Chloe, Blue Fifth Review, Blueline, Blue Jew Yorker, Bryant Literary Review, Berkeley Poetry Review, Blood Root, Broome Review, Breadcrumb Scabs, Coachella Review, Coe Review, Cosmopsis, Comstock Review, Clean Sheets, Diode, Evening Street Review, Edison Review, Eclectica, Earth's Daughters, Eloquent Atheist, EarthSpeak, Future Cycle, FRiGG, Ghoti, J Journal, Kiss-Fist, Loch Raven Review, Leveler, Literary Bohemian, Mochilla Review, Mamazine.com, New Plains Review, New Verse News, Off the Coast, Ozone Park, Pure Francis, Physiognomy in Letters, PoetryRepairs, ProsePoems, Picayune Literary Magazine, Poemeleon, Sawbuck, SLAB, Stirring, Sendero, Stone's Throw, Spillway, Shortpoem. org, Subtle Tea, Switched-on Gutenberg, Slant, The Sun, The Scrambler, Third Wednesday, Toasted Cheese, Two Review, 2River View, Thieves Jargon, Thick with Conviction, Terrain. org, Upstreet, Verdad, White Pelican Review, Wild Goose Review, Whirlwind Review.

CONTENTS

I. UNLIKELY LOVES

II. AGONIES AND ORGASMS

III. HEAVEN AND EARTH

IV. LETTING GO

I. UNLIKELY LOVES

UNCANNY

People look like people
and places look like places
and everything rhymes a little
and has been said before.

Bob Dylan in his late 60s
looks a lot like my mother.
It's partly the nose,
partly the big hair.

Déjà vu is the French I knew
before I knew French.
It's nice to meet you,
I've loved you ever since you were born

and probably longer than that.
Can't ken it, canst thou, Kenneth?
Nope. That shit cannot be taught.
This is the poem I have wished I'd written

ever since I read it.

LITTLE THINGS

Me and Beth Jeannette had a little thing.
This was a long time ago when my
thing was little and I didn't know anything
about such things. Somehow we ended up
upstairs in her bedroom on her bed
with her face very close to mine and a little
pimply. Her eyes were soft, her hands were
busy. My hands were folded politely
in my lap, as though waiting for tea or
poetry. My eyes, roaming the walls, found
an M.C. Escher print with tessellating
staircases, and climbed them peripherally
while Beth continued to block my view
with her nose. In the end, our little thing
was like those staircases—it went nowhere
though it seemed to be going somewhere,
especially when she touched my thing and I
had to go to the bathroom. All these years later
I look back on that little thing with fondness,
tenderness, and a little sadness, as though
I were looking back from deep within infinity
at my first tender, tentative tessellations.

Paul Hostovsky

EXEGESIS

We couldn't have been more than twelve
or thirteen, sitting on that green bench in the late
sixties or early seventies, me and Michael Zucker
who was much more savvy and world-weary
than I, when I asked him to please explain
the meaning of the words to a song by Carly
Simon, who was simply gorgeous—that much was
plain—after we'd resolved the essential question
of whether or not she was wearing a bra
in that photo of her with the blue top and thick
lips on her album cover. "I don't get it," I said.
"'You're so vain. You probably think this song is about you.'
But the song IS about him, isn't it?" I asked Zucker,
holding my palm up in the air like one who is
trying to ascertain the truth about whether or not
it has started to rain. Zucker looked away then,
gingerly fingering the green slats, as though he were
reading the carved names of the lovers and obscenities
tactually. Then he took a deep breath and exhaled
miserably, took the album cover out of my hands
and gazed awhile at Carly Simon who was gorgeous,
famous, braless, and older than me and Zucker put together.
"That's the point," he said. "She's in love with him."

GERMAN

I thought it sounded strong, impressive, Germanic,
to say: "I have to go to German now." I imagined
my friends all staring admiringly at my back
as I walked industriously down the tessellating hallway
to German, my posture slightly straighter, my rucksack
slightly heavier with Dieter and Petra inside dialoging
about Bratwurst and Goethe and Turkish guest workers.
I could recite "Der Erlkoenig" by heart, and my r's
were perfect drum solos. Nancy Baum sat in the seat in front of me
and pretended not to hear when I whispered: *Ich liebe dich*
into her umlaut—that pair of moles on her left earlobe.
I thought it sounded romantic, Germanic, productive
as a cough. Frau Spier thought so too, for she asked me
to repeat it for the benefit of the whole class. Nancy's
earlobes blushed then, and her umlaut looked
like two watermelon seeds. Later that semester
I translated one of Rilke's sonnets to Orpheus,
the one about the tree and the ear. My translation
employed an umlaut where no previous translator
had ever thought to. I thought it was brilliant, subtle,
Orphic. I published it in our high school lit mag
and waited. I waited twenty years. Then, suddenly,
there she was in front of me again, with her back to me
at the reunion, lifting a mixed drink to her lips with a slender
ringless hand at the bar, the umlaut right where I'd left it.
I whispered: *Ich liebe dich,* and she turned around, the wall
finally down, smiling a smile as wide as East and West.

Paul Hostovsky

KISS

On the train
heading south
all the seats
facing north
like the meeting
of east and west
our heads turning slowly
on the headrests
toward each other
like two completely
different ways of life
coming together
on either side
of a body
of water
our eyes like
messengers
studying each other
from opposite shores
then entering
that body
wading through it
chest-high
exchanging aloft
the moist and crumpled
messages

THE DEBATE AT DUFFY'S

She said that sex was a yearning of the soul.
He said it was a very compelling argument
of the body, a compulsion. She said it was
a *spiritual* compulsion. He said it was nothing
if not carnal, *carni,* meat. This conversation
took place in a bar. The background music was
so loud it was in the foreground. The bodies
on the dance floor were moving in ways that
would interest even the dead if they could only
remember how to live. There was a baseball game
playing on television. On the table were two
empty glasses, and the bottle's green phallus
which she took in her hand and pulled toward her,
pulling him toward her as she poured them both
another drink. He drank deeply, felt the spirit
filling his cup. Then he looked into her eyes and saw
that she was beautiful, sexy, and at the bottom
of the 9th, suddenly, surprisingly, irrevocably, right.

Paul Hostovsky

TO A LANDSCAPER

You smell like a lawnmower, love.
Come sit your grassy ass down
on the bed. I want to taste the green
sweat spreading like wealth all over
your body, the lawns of the rich and
gasoline commingling on your skin and
bones. I want to feel the suburbs
rub off on us like the laughing poor
streaking through the formal gardens
of the scowling rich, the fine gold pollen
sticking to our nakedness like sex on sex,
our own bed filthy and rich beneath
the well-oiled machine of our lovemaking.

THE AFFAIR IN THE OFFICE

It belonged to all of us in a way
because we all shared
in the surprise
that it existed at all,
and also, privately, in the thrill
of the two lovers
(none more surprised than they)
who'd worked together in the same sad office
with all of us for all
these years, and both of them married,
and both unhappily. It was
a sad office, like so many
sad offices, full of the inexorable sadness
of cubicles, and computers, and empty
of love. Or so we thought. For no one
saw it growing—it must have
gotten in through a high
bit of laughter in the lunchroom,
then a glancing away
and a looking back again, the way
it sometimes does. And when it got out
in whispers around the water cooler
we all drank from it,
we drank it in, and in this way
it refreshed us, and amazed us,
and belonged to us because
we all took it home, took it
with us in the car, or on the train, sat with it
in rush hour, shaking our heads as though
we were listening to music, and in a way
we were listening to music,
shaking our heads and smiling,
looking out the window, fingers drumming.

Paul Hostovsky

BATTLING THE WIND AND EVERYTHING ELSE

My neighbor—the one with the flagpole
and the flag, and the pickup truck
and the patriotic bumper sticker and the perfect
lawn, and the leaf-blower with the power pack—
never seems to see me when I wave to him.
In fact, I am trying to get his attention
right now, but his eyes are on the enemy,
the leaves. He is aiming the long barrel
of his leaf-blower at them, and blowing
them away. But the wind is counting its money
and throwing it away all over his lawn.
He is Sisyphus pushing one red leaf or another
up the berm of a perfect lawn forever. And I feel
sorry for him, the way I might feel sorry for
a large carnivorous bird in a shrinking ecosystem
on the nature channel. I know when he looks at me
he sees a guy who is half-assedly, half-heartedly
raking the leaves around on a disgrace-of-a-lawn
the way a kid pushes the peas around on his dinner plate
with his fork, trying to make it look like there are fewer
peas than before, when really there are still the exact
same number of peas; and he sees the leaves messing up
his lawn as *my* leaves, because *his* leaves are all in order—
he sees to that. So the ones that are crossing the border
and have no right to be here and should just go back
to where they came from, must be *mine*. I see this all
written on his face as he grits his teeth and stares
the dancing leaves down, then blows them up
over the edge of his property. But they keep on
dancing back again because there's a party
going on here, and the wind is counting its money

and throwing it away. So I walk right up to him—
I get right in his face so he can't not see me,
and I wave hello. He disengages his leaf-blower,
after revving it a few times first at the intersection
of our meeting. And I say to him, "I've been trying
to get your attention." And he says, "You got it."
And I say, "How you doing?" And he says, "Battling
the wind and everything else." And I say, "I can see that."
And he says, "How *you* doing?" And I say, "Good. Good."

Paul Hostovsky

BLUES HARP

More like a cross between a saxophone
and a five-alarm fire
than a Hohner harmonica
small enough to fit in the palm of her hand
or breast pocket. He was thinking
the fact that she even had breasts
was almost completely beside the point.
Almost. For he had never
heard anyone, much less a woman,
play harp like that. It was
powerful, intelligent, sexy,
downright athletic the way she ran
her tongue up and down it, breathing
hard into the bullet mike, Chicago-style,
trading licks with the rhythm guitarist
center-stage, bending the notes into
shapes that conjured up for him the beautiful
catastrophes of train wrecks. He wanted
to get her alone after the set, out behind
the club, and in the darkness whip out his
own harmonica, and play a long train with her,
show her his rhythms by starting out slow,
then building speed underneath her
while she whistled and steamed and moaned
on top, letting her juggle the high notes
like so many birds in the hand, so many
waves upon waves, while he chugged along
steady and low, running like clockwork, letting her lead,
letting her go, letting her, letting her, letting her.

OPEN

She left everything open—
windows, doors, drawers, cabinets,
the little cap on the tube of toothpaste,
letting the air in, letting the bugs in, letting
everything in—while he, on the other hand,

was a firm believer in twisties
and double knots, double bagging and double
checking to make sure the door was
double locked. You could say
she trusted while he trussed. He wanted

to bind her to him, with that wedding band
on the one hand; on the other, she wanted
to keep their relationship open. "The heart
must remain open," she said. He closed
his eyes and exhaled miserably. "And where

does that leave us?" he asked, and opened
his eyes and saw that she was sitting
close to him on the couch, her mouth slightly
open, as if to say "kiss me" without saying it.

Paul Hostovsky

DERMATOLOGIST

I think I was in the fourth grade
when I first learned the word epidermis.
I went up to each of my friends in turn
and said, "Your epidermis is showing,"
and each looked down to see if his fly was open
because epidermis and penis have the same
happy ending. I knew back then already
that knowing more than others about
the largest organ in the human body
puts you at an advantage. "The functions
of the skin," I would say to my date, years later
in medical school, as we sat in my car outside
the movie theater, "include absorption,
excretion, insulation, synthesis of vitamin D,
and *sensation*." Then I'd demonstrate
this last function by touching her lightly
on the arm, and then the cheek—"Do you
follow, love?"—and if she said yes,
on the breast. And if she said no,
I would tell her about the 50 million bacteria
living on the surface of each square inch
of human skin, which no amount of cleaning
can remove. Then I'd smile a little sadly,
put the car in drive, and tell her that moist
and dry skin, ecologically speaking, are as different
as rainforests and deserts, and without elaborating,
drive her back through the world to her dormitory.

SNAIL MAIL

Two dragonflies hover
in an envelope of air—
a flying fuck

outside the new P.O.
which is for lovers
only.

The old bald eagle
is retired, the whole
idea of flight

entirely revised.
Snail me a rectangle, love.
Let your tongue

(delicacy I'm dreaming of)
secrete a slimy path along
its flap, its one

vestigial wing.
Pop it in a blue
drop on any corner

bearing the new triptych logo:
the conch, the whelk, the periwinkle,
inching along in reverse

psychological order,
symbolizing the involute
progress of arousal.

Paul Hostovsky

Slow is in. Slow
is good in love and slow
dancing, long and wet

kisses. Email
is for exes
and execs. We know

better, don't we, love?
We'll take that letter.
We'll take forever any day.

ARS P.O.

A poem should have
at least one good list.
Anything liquid, fragile, perishable,
or potentially hazardous?
A poem should be
suspicious
as a package you might put
into the hands of
unsuspecting others.
Can you be trusted?
Can they be trusted?
You can receive a thing
without opening it.
You can reject a thing
without opening it. You can
read a poem by holding it up to the light,
holding it up to your ear
and giving it a shake
to see what shifts. You can
even walk away from it
and come back to it later
to see if it has changed
you, opened you. Oh my
bearer of rectangles,
if I could tell you
how to tell the pure
money of the poems
from all the other rectangles
in your little square truck
with its picture
of flight on both flanks
and also in the back,
if I could show you

Paul Hostovsky

how to feel it
through the envelope,
like a Braille letter,
like someone else's
goose bumps in your hands,
worth its weight in
transport of a kind I cannot
teach you how to make your own,
though you steal it,
though you open every
letter, oh my poor
letter carrier, rich already
with the handling of it,
though you look for it in all
four corners
of its own sumptuous
destitute world
which is thinner than paper,
which is air itself,
air from the country
of someone else's
mouth, oh my beautiful
mailman, I would,
I would.

RECONNAISSANCE

He couldn't stop looking
at the photograph
of his wife from long ago,
her school picture
in which she was only 12
and had no body,

only a head
and a neck, a red
shirt collar opening
onto the invisible country
that was just beginning
to develop below the border.

Here his imagination
pitched its tent. Here
the scouts of his eyes
kept returning

to her eyes,
the facts of them,
which hadn't changed at all
in all that time.

And here was her mouth,
which he had kissed
a hundred million times,

before he kissed it once,
a girlish smile
playing at the lips
some game of its own
imagining.

Paul Hostovsky

UNLIKELY LOVE

I saw him today in the Public Garden,
walking briskly and alone, all bundled up
against the snow and against the fact
that you don't love him anymore.
How heavy his heart, I thought, and yet
he stepped so lightly, looked so self-possessed,
walking down the narrow pathway between
the benches. I knew he was suffering because
you told me how he had cried. And as he lifted
a gloved hand to adjust his ear-muffs, I felt
something for him, something in that moment
that I knew you wouldn't understand if I tried
explaining it to you tonight when I saw you—
because I still don't understand it myself—
it was something like pathos, but something more
like love, really—I felt a sudden rush of love
for this man whom you don't love anymore,
and haven't loved for a long time, as you told me
after that first time we kissed, back in October…
Now it's the middle of February and I wonder
about him, wonder if his pain has stayed the same,
or gotten worse, or better, these five months I've been
making love to you without thinking of him—
and why should I think of him? But then, suddenly,
there he is, crossing my path today, looking
terribly alone, but also—I don't know—girded
against the cold, against the loneliness, and I wanted
to follow him, not to where he was going but
how he was going. A part of me wanted to be him.
A part of me wants to be with you, but a part of me
wants to be with him, head down in the wind, clenching
myself against the cold loneliness raining down.

IF NOT FOR STEPHEN DUNN

This poem is not for Stephen Dunn.
It's for the one whose Stephen Dunn I stole
out of a hospital waiting room
when no one was looking,

when he or she—when *you*
(I like to imagine you're a she)
got up to go to the toilet maybe,
and sat there thinking
(I like to imagine you sitting on a toilet, thinking)

about a poem by Stephen Dunn
lying open and face-down
out on the waiting-room table where you left it
a little naively perhaps

among the magazines—
an expensive cut of meat on a bed of jelly beans,
cooling on the sill of the world

where I found it
when I entered feeling ravenous
and symptomatic,
thinking

you only live once,
and feeling
justified in stealing this book,
stuffing it into my yellow backpack like enough
food for one person for one year.

A year later I returned it.
It was one week after 9/11. Policemen
were stationed in the hospital corridors then.

Paul Hostovsky

I must have looked guilty, shady, unshaven,
like a terrorist trying to plant
fifty stolen poems by Stephen Dunn
on a waiting room table full of magazines,

for they stopped me
just inside the doorway,
and asked me politely and dead
seriously

to remove my yellow backpack.
Two secretaries, a nurse, several patients
(I like to imagine a liver recipient
sitting somewhere among them) looked on

as two thick and inarticulate
constabulary hands,
trembling, drew out
and held up under a light, under a nose,

this bundle of devices
with enough combined force to take
at least 3 lives—
yours, mine and Dunn's—
completely by surprise.

II. AGONIES AND ORGASMS

LOVE AND DEATH

I love sitting here opposite you in our underwear,
talking about death. We sip our tea together
after making love on your all-encompassing couch,
and I assert there really is no death, there is only

life, which has no opposite because
it is all-encompassing. We hug and kiss some more
and you tell me about your sister-in-law's mother
who recently died of pancreatic cancer. It took

three months, you say. She was fine one day and the next
in so much pain that three hours of that kind of pain,
not to mention three days or three weeks or three
months would be more than you or I or anyone

in the world should have to bear. I lean over
and give you a peck, and go into the kitchen to make
more tea. I stand there looking at the flame for a long time—
maybe three minutes—before the water starts to boil.

MOTHER'S DAY

It's Mother's Day and I need a mother.
My mother is dead and my grandmother
is dead too. And the mother of my children
is "the mother of my children," and we don't
talk. I'm all dressed up with no mother to go.
I have a card and some flowers and I'm walking
around, looking at the mothers in the windows,
the shop windows and restaurant windows,
with their husbands and their children. And I feel
motherless. And I know I look motherless, too.
I know in spite of my card and flowers and cow-
lick and new shoes, people see right through me.
They see I'm an imposter. A poseur. A mother-
fucker who would steal your mother and help you
look for her. What was she wearing? Is she young
or old? Large breasts or small? Of course it's a
Sunday in May, so there's all this pollen in the air,
so there's all this sex in the air, and the motherless
trees are standing erect in the breeze, shivering with
pleasure. And the ejaculations of the lost and laughing
mothers are pealing in the Sunday air, like a summons.

Paul Hostovsky

OKAY

I'm an English major okay
so when you say okay and that's all you say
in reply to my much longer
email about you and me and what happened
and what happens and what will happen
I don't know how to read your okay okay
I mean I'm scanning the y and the a for some kind of
meaning lurking in the choice to spell okay
okay instead of ok or o.k.
or OK or O.K. as though
you might be spelling something out for me here
and then there's that exclamation point
which follows your okay and probably doesn't
warrant the kind of assiduous exegesis
I've already performed on it in my head
analyzing it for voice and tone and register
and volume and pitch and number
because because because
because of the wonderful things we've done
together in all kinds of weather and places and positions
and durations and voices and volumes
and although I know that isn't the point
of your exclamation point it's all I have to work with here
outside of your okay
and everything your okay isn't saying
which is what it's leaving out
which I know from having read one or two
hundred thousand poems in my lifetime
is just as important as what's left in
but what I want to know is
okay where does that leave us?

50-YEAR-OLD CIRCUITRY

He looks at all the beautiful women
especially all the young beautiful women
especially all the old enough to be her father
beautiful women and he feels a little
ashamed of himself
but he also feels that what he feels
is a sign
that he's alive
in fact it's the only he's alive sign that's still
got all the bulbs burning
brightly inside of it
so whenever he sees a beautiful young woman
like his daughter's friend Bethany for example
whose body is a precocious
light bulb and whose face is a pure
light
he can't look at her and he can't stop looking at her
and his eyes turn into neon I'm alive signs
alternating with the all night
SEX signs flashing in the red light district
behind his vanishing hairline
so the combined effect is a kind of
I'm STILL fucking ALIVE sign
which lights him up
and turns her off
and turns his daughter against him

PEARL IN BUBBLE WRAP

She's pretty deaf and pretty blind and pretty
in an octogenarian sort of way, her hair completely
white, and pulled back tight from her high smooth forehead.
If staring at the blind is rude, I must be downright
scurrilous. Scurrilous piety, this kneeling down in front of
her wheelchair, to tie her shoelace which has come untied,
then sitting back down across from her to stare
some more. *Snap, snap, snap,* goes the bubble wrap
in her mottled fist, her fingers thirsting after the next
and the next explosion under thumb. I can see on her face
how sensual, how satisfying this sensation is for her
whose sensations are mostly tactile now that she's pretty
deaf and pretty blind and pretty alone here at the nursing home
where they can't communicate with her. So they give her
the bubble wrap, lots of it, to keep her busy, happy, maybe even
joyful, bursting joy's grape over and over, getting her
eighty-year-old ya-ya's out in her wheelchair parked
in front of my eyes. And I can't help wondering
how much bubble wrap she's gone through in the days
and weeks and months she's been here, how many miles of it
she's consumed. She's probably been to the moon and back
on her fingertips, dancing along the backs of these plastic
turtles, leaping across these disappearing stones, these rivers
of bubble wrap, oceans of bubble wrap. "Pearl!" I shout
into her good ear, the one with the cochlear implant. "I have
to get going now!" She looks up vaguely, pauses briefly from
the pursuit of more pleasure in her lap. I give her a kiss
and head for the elevator. Once inside, I push the Lobby button
several times before it lights up. Then I worry the Braille beside it
with my index finger, all the long way down to the street.

LOOKING AT BOOBS WITH AUNT EDIE

Me and my Aunt Edie are looking
at my parents' wedding album.
My parents are dead, my Aunt Edie
is living with dementia, I'm fifty
and twice divorced—just to give you
an idea, a preamble. On the first page
a photo of my mother and grandmother.
Aunt Edie's short-term memory is shot,
but she can still remember the name
of her 4th grade teacher, her best friend
from camp, her great Aunt Millie, Uncle
Donald, and the exact number of the house
on Observanten Straat where she lived
in Maastricht until she was eight: #26. "Hey,
look how busty Savtah looks," she says,
and we stare awhile at my grandmother's
boobs. I smile, nod, and turn the page
to a photo of my mother and grandfather
walking down the aisle arm-in-arm. "Hey,
look how pointy Reggie's boobs are here,"
says Aunt Edie. And I can't help noticing
the theme that's developing page by page,
breast by breast. And I'm wondering if
this is a side of Aunt Edie that was always
there, only covered up, inhibited, corseted
like her own ample breasts ("which were
always much bigger than your mother's,"
she says to me now) and only coming out
in her late seventies, now that she's forgotten
the reason for keeping it hid. Whatever
the reason, her celebration of the bosoms
of the women of my family is making me
squirm. That's when she looks up, adjusts

Paul Hostovsky

her bra strap, fixes me with a penetrating hazel arrow, and says, "If I didn't know you better, nephew, I'd say you were blushing."

ORGASMS IN AUTUMN

I used to think spring was the sexiest season.
But now I think it's fall
with all its burning smells
and the musculature
of the impatient trees with their
red pants down around their knees
already—and all this talk of peak
foliage, which reminds me of all the talk
of orgasms, which are both the point and
so beside the point. I mean look
how beautiful. I mean feel how impossible—
everything building, everything climbing toward a high
tingling, a ringing in the ears, a flying
down through the world from the highest
branches. When I was a kid
I used to stand with my back to the trunks of trees
(a kind of renunciation
of hide-and-seek) and count
with eyes wide open
the number of leaves falling right now,
then take off running, darting zigzag,
trying to catch them, to take them,
snatch them out of the air mid-dance before
they could touch the ground. I played that game
for hours and hours, years—
sweaty and breathless, happy
just to be catching the falling beauty
in my hands, then letting it go, throwing it back
into the world.

GET WELL CARD IN CARDIOLOGY

The beautiful nurses of history
are all out in the corridor,
nursing. If you push the call button
their beautiful voices
will ask you what you want.
If you tell them you want *them*
they will give you their beautiful
laughter and a gentle
rebuke. If you keep on pushing the call button
they will send in the plain nurses
whose voices are also beautiful
to confuse you. If you close your eyes and just
keep on pushing the call button for all it's worth
they will take the call button away from you.
The world is like that.
What you need is one of those crazy great ideas
men get when they're in love,
the kind that just might work,
the kind that makes a man great
and gets him the woman. History
is full of crazy great ideas. Borrow one.
You can do better than pushing your call button
and pulling your catheter out.
Very mediocre ideas, my friend.
You just keep on imagining all day
every day of your convalescence
the beautiful nurses of history
lining up in the corridor outside your room,
and you will get better soon,
because history is on your side,
and exercising your imagination
is not only good for your heart,
it's good for God and country.
Repeat after me: I pledge allegiance
to beauty.

FLOWERS

On the first day of school in the second grade
Amy Steinberg is telling Tammy Beale
that Amy'll be her best friend if Tammy will
show us all her vagina first. I'm eight
and feeling rather sorry for Tammy but
never having seen one I also feel
that feeling sorry for Tammy shouldn't preclude
my getting a good look in case she should.

Later, as I position my head on the floor
among the other heads all looking up—
our bodies fanning out like the spokes of a wheel,
and Tammy standing over us on two chairs—
I think to myself: it looks like a closed flower,
and we an open one, maybe, to her looking down.

Paul Hostovsky

POP FLIES

I'm hitting a few pop flies to my friend Richard
when along comes Stephen Cutler, the toughest kid
in the neighborhood, walking his Doberman pinscher.
He asks me gruffly for a turn at bat, and the Doberman
growls. So I motion to Richard out in left field
to move farther back. Then I silently surrender
the bat and the ball. A wind dies on the schoolyard.

He tosses the ball up, swings at the exact second
that the Doberman, sniffing a game, jumps for the ball
and catches the bat in its head—suddenly there's blood
everywhere, the Doberman's seizing, dying, Cutler's crying,
and Richard's running for help, growing smaller and smaller,
like he's chasing a pop fly that went sailing over his head,
over the fence, houses, treetops—a pop fly, flying.

THE PLACE OF LITERATURE

Mr. Gordon was perhaps a little tipsy
at the awards ceremony, perhaps a little
scornful of the football coach's ode
to yardage, the basketball coach's
paeons to the MVPs, the music teacher's touting
her flautist, the science teacher his
scion of Einstein. So when Mr. Gordon
got up to give the literary magazine award
to me, he lurched a little drunkenly, swayed
a little imperceptibly, steeply rocking in his
moment on stage. Not to be outdone,
he said in his opinion I was probably
the greatest poet writing in English anywhere today—
and a gasp went up from the high school auditorium,
then murmurs of admiration and disbelief and
mutiny spread through the audience as I rose
to accept Mr. Gordon's slightly exaggerated
handshake. Then he kissed me on the mouth,
and raised my hand above my head in the manner
of referees and prizefighters, grinning glaringly
over at the football coach, and nodding trochaically.

Paul Hostovsky

CHILDHOOD

This is an imaginary story with real names in it.
Billy Most's mother's name was Myrna.
Myrna Most is a great name, and no one
was innocent, least of all Billy, whom we called

Toad. Maybe we'd have called him Mole
if we knew they were called moles. They speckled
his face and neck and made him look like a toad. In the end
I'm just a man looking to buy back his childhood

home. I press the doorbell gingerly. I come from
gum surgery. Gingivitis. Myrna is the realtor.
She walks me through the branching rooms, narrating.
I press the periodontal packing with my tongue,

and it resembles the flashing on the roof
in the angle where the roof meets the chimney
which is old and red and missing a few teeth.
The neighbor on the left was Mrs. Nad.

Toad called her Nag. I, too, disliked her.
But I was neutral in the turf war between
the sidewalk and the curb, where Nag had planted
sod, and tied some string on sticks around it

to keep us kids off it as we walked
to school and home. Toad always trampled it
on purpose, kicked it up maliciously, goose-
stepping, heels digging in: oops, oops, oops,

the crescent divots flying up like commas
punctuating the blank air. Suddenly Nag
comes hurtling down her front steps like
an exclamation point in an apron

and runs him through, and drags us *both*
by our ears over to my house (because Nag was a great
name and no one was innocent). But then she wavers,
as if wondering how to ring the bell with her hands full

of ears. Meanwhile Myrna recites certain details,
expunges certain others. I listen politely, tonguing
the wound in my head. And all of this feels like being
walked through my own body by a specialist,

a prostitute, say, with a very professional air
and expertise concerning this most intimate
part of me, where I haven't set foot in years,
not since I moved away to a state with a name that

sounded like another country, Pennsylvania
or California. Incredibly, Nag begins weeping,
and lets go of our ears, and turns and walks
away. She seems to grow very old. She begins

picking up the divots one by one, like scalps
of her great, great grandparents murdered in their sleep
by Toad Indians. She piles them in her apron, kneels
on the sidewalk, fits them gingerly back into the earth.

Paul Hostovsky

This would be the perfect place to insert
an insight. Some lesson learned, some observation made
concerning friends and neighbors, life and death
and childhood. This would be the perfect place. Let us

pray. We kneel down beside her, to help her. Toad
returns to rake her leaves in the fall, shovels
her walk in winter. He buys a fleet of lawnmowers.
I move away to another country. Myrna Most

sells another house. The For Sale sign dangles
from the yellow stake in the mouth of my aching
front yard, a little cement in the hole. It's early
April. I can't believe what they're asking.

THE GOOD FIGHT

Which one
is the good fight
anyway?
Isn't it the good guy
kicking butt but
a little reluctantly
because he's good
and hates to have to,
but since no one else would,
and wrong would just go
on unrighted,
he steps up to the plate
and takes a few good swings
and puts that baby to bed? Go
fuck yourself, you said
and have said nothing else
all day. Now it's night
and your silence is still
that choked, caked, kill-
all-the-motherfuckers-take-
no-prisoners kind
you have honed to a fine
squint. But I only
meant to point out
what was wrong—
to right it. I don't know much
but I know I love
your butt more than God
or country,
and when we fight
it hurts me right
here—right

Paul Hostovsky

here. And now
I think the good fight
is the one we get through
quickly, get to the other side of
with nothing dead or otherwise
irreparable floating
in the churning reddish
air we part like a sea
miraculously
finding our way back
to each other's
arms.

ITALIAN CUISINE

I'm visiting my half-sister Olga
in Bologna. She's 45 and married
to an Italian. I'm 15, American, and the only
Italian word I know besides spaghetti

is baloney. My family
history reads like one of those libretti
where everyone is falling in love and jumping
out of windows. Alleluia, Allioop!

My nephew Dario, 4 years older than me (go
figure), takes me to a party on the Via Faenza
where everyone is smoking and eating
pot brownies. They take turns

practicing their English on the American.
I feel famous, then exploited.
Someone is telling a long hilarious joke
in Italian. All of my interpreters

are cracking up and rolling on the floor,
mute with laughter. I smile helplessly,
sweep the floor with my eyes for the dropped
English. It evaporates like water in a pot

of giddy spaghetti. The brownies kick in.
I float to the window, look out at the porticos leapfrogging
to infinity through the streets of Bologna.
I close my eyes and see

Olga in her kitchen, holding a rolling pin;
my father in Prague, holding a cigarette
like a leaky pen, pointing it drippingly up
at a portrait of Jan Masaryk who

jumped (go figure) out a window.
I see Wendy Iazzoni back in Jersey, smiling
at the end of a long tunnel in space—
I can see the gap between her teeth perfectly,

I can even see the gap between the buttons
of her blouse, which was always space enough—
when Dario taps my scapula and we lapse
into English. Back at Olga's

it's rigatoni for dinner—
little fluted tunnels floating
in a white wine sauce. I'm still
stoned. I hold one drippingly up

to my left eye while closing
my right: Olga floats into focus
glaring like the Inquisition at Dario
who's holding a rigatoni telescope

of his own, peering through it across
the dinner table at me, the American
Galileo. "Nevertheless,
it moves," I intone. He explodes

into exorbitant laughter.

PRAGUE

They wanted to show me the Castle, but I was more interested in
the doorknobs, which were mostly levers instead of knobs, and the
toilets which were mostly not in the bathrooms, but in little rooms
beside the bathrooms, and the *pater noster* elevators which were
left over from communism and had no doors or buttons and never
stopped moving so you had to leap in or leap out when they got to
your floor. And the squirrels which were mostly red or black instead
of gray. And the blue streaks of the thieving socialist magpies with
their clicking metered phrases, which sounded a lot like their
cousins, the American blue jays back home. And the fact that things
here in general somehow seemed a lot more substantial, the bread
for example, and the soups, and the eyebrows of the grandmothers,
and the beer, and the coffee, and the buildings, and the rooftops
which were mostly red instead of gray. And the heft of the coins,
and the blue of the sky. And the beauty of the women, all those
beautiful substantial Czech women, none of whom, I would have
bet my return ticket, was headed for the Castle or the Old Jewish
Cemetery.

Paul Hostovsky

MOZART IN YOUR ARMPIT

A winter morning, and *Cosi*
is frozen from being in the car all night,
so at first the music sounds like
an aria trying to sing its way out

of a snow bank. I eject the tape
and stick it in my armpit on
my aunt's advice: "Keep it there
till the voices warm up—

Mozart in your armpit, he'd
have loved the thought of that," she says
as we drive off to the hospital together
talking about Mozart and opera and phantom

pain. Her wheelchair, minus the leg rests,
is propped at a slightly bewildered angle
in the backseat of my Toyota.
"It's all about sex," she says

as I steer with one hand, trying
to reposition Mozart
still thawing, with the other.
"*Cosi*'s all about doing it,

and thinking about doing it,
and thinking about doing it with somebody else.
Forget about learning Italian.
If you love the music already

the words won't make you love it more.
Take it from me, I have no legs,
but don't I still have the pain?"
I tell her, with all due respect for her legs

and her pain, that I fail to see the connection
between learning Italian and having an amputation.
That's when a painful silence swallows the car whole.
I dip my hand in my shirt, but the tape's still cold.

"Not *an* amputation. Eight! Count 'em:
this little piggy, then his neighbor, then
the whole damn block, then up to the knee.
Then a year later, all over again

on the other side of the street."
She slaps her left stump, then her right,
and it looks like a flam on a pair of bongos,
or a rim-shot after the punch line

of a bad joke in the Catskills.
"I'm talking about feeling.
You lack Italian. I lack legs.
You still feel pleasure. I pain.

Phantom pain they call it. Mozart
knew about phantom pain, how it
isn't what it feels like, how it
drags you down to hell with it in the end.

You think you've taken care of a thing,
severed it from yourself for good—
then there it is again, what can't be.
And feeling more like itself than ever.

Listen, you don't need the words to know
when the music has changed; when the pain
has turned to pleasure; the pleasure
to pain.

It's all vowels anyway—one
long dilating Italian vowel
sliding into another: orgasm,
agony, orgasm, agony again.

You get my point now, nephew?
Good, now be a good boy
and put in the tape.
Give me Mozart while he's hot."

III.   HEAVEN AND EARTH

HAND CREAM

If you look up Messiah it says
something about being anointed.
If you look up anointed it says
something about smearing or rubbing
oil or unguents. If you look up unguents
it says they're like ointments or salves.
Jesus Salves would be a great name
for a hand cream, I believe. I believe
hand eczema is one of a dozen
skin diseases that got lumped together
under leprosy in the New Testament.
I believe a little hand cream everyday
goes a long way toward healing dry skin,
and if you squeeze the tube a little too hard
and too much unguent squirts out,
you can do what Jesus did: spread
the wealth around, anoint yourself and
others, rub some on your forearms
and their forearms, on their faces and tired
necks and shoulders and backs, the whole
body of Christ. If you look up holiness
it says something about being set apart
for sanctification. If you look up sanctification
it says something about being set apart
for holiness. One hand washing the other
just like in Jesus' day. But if you look up
salvation, surprisingly it doesn't say anything
about Jesus, or salves, or the Messiah.
It talks about our liberation from clinging
to the world of appearances, and the illusions
of sickness, pain, and death. A final, joyful
union with ultimate reality. Really good stuff.

THE QUINTESSENTIAL IMPOTENCE POEM

Quintessence is the fifth and highest essence
that permeates all nature and is the substance
that the heavenly bodies are composed of. Impotence

is the state of no sex in heaven. Or if there is
sex in heaven, it will technically have to be masturbation,
because everyone is one and the same in heaven.

Hell is having nothing to read but your own
poems. A psychiatrist is someone with a hanging
psychiatric shingle outside his door. A prostitute

is someone who sucks dick for a living.
A dangling participle is a relative clause
in an ambiguous sentence, or it's a life sentence

in a man with erectile dysfunction. For example:
"Jerry Remy hit an RBI single off Haas's leg,
which rolled into right field." You would think

the leg rolled into right field. You would think
getting to first base with a girl would give you
a boner as hard as a baseball bat. All we know

is that Remy got to first base and someone
scored. Whoever it was, he must have been very
happy. He probably got an erection. He probably got

a raise in pay and self-esteem, and he probably
had an erector set when he was a kid. My mother
never bought me an erector set. And my father never

learned to speak English very well. He thought a home run was something you did when your mother forgot to pick you up after your baseball game.

OPEN

I'm open to god but I don't like capitalizing
on god. I mean I'll open the door
to the Jehovah's Witnesses, but I won't
let them dominate the conversation.
"For what profiteth it a man," I ask them,
"if he gains salvation but loses
the remote?" They smile uncomfortably
as I turn and head into the kitchen,
returning with the longest carving knife
in the drawer. Their eyes get very big
and they start back-pedaling toward the door…
"It's a double-edged sword," I tell them,
"this war between the spirit and the flesh."
Then I prostrate myself in front of
the couch, and cast around underneath it
till the knife touches up against something
I hope is the remote. "The way a life of renunciation
touches up against something one hopes
is the soul…" I say to my well-dressed
guests hurtling down my front steps now
two at a time, not hearing me at all,
though my door remains open, my cheek turned
to the cool hardwood floor, and I'm fishing
around for something lost, contemplating all this dust.

Paul Hostovsky

GOD, DAN

I was a junior and Dan was a senior
drug addict in the school of arts and sciences. Neil
Young was a prolific songwriter with no
allegiances, except for the music. I had never
done cocaine before, so while he was cutting it
on the square mirror on top of the dresser, I put on
the record, and asked him what kind of shape
I would be in for class at two o'clock. He said
it was an aphrodisiac, so go figure. He was
cutting class himself and meeting his girlfriend
at one-thirty, because all it made him want to do
was fuck. I didn't have a girlfriend. I had a Comparative
Religion class at two o'clock, and now I was thinking
twice about getting high before God and
man. But Dan was in a hurry, and he handed me
the rolled-up twenty which I knew enough to
stick inside my nose and aim at the nearest
cloud-row reflected in the square lake on top
of the dresser—and sniff vigorously. Then Dan
was saying something about making love
as he left the room, and Neil was saying something
about needing someone to love him the whole
day through, and I was alone with God and no one
to talk to about God, when the coke kicked in.
Thank God for Dan, who came back looking
for his twenty. "I don't think God created the world,"
I said to him as he scooped up the bill and licked
the top of the dresser with his tongue, as an afterthought.
"In fact, I doubt He even knows we're here."
"Thank God for that," said Dan, "because all I want
to do in the world is snort cocaine and rub my cock."
I loved his honesty. I told him I would try to weave it in
to my paper on Abraham. "You need to get laid, man,"

said Dan. "Old man, take a look at my life," said Neil.
I sat down at the typewriter and began: " 'Here am I,'
said Abraham to God." "I'm out of here," said Dan.

Paul Hostovsky

THE SELF

It was a Buddhist lecture on the Self.
There must have been fifty people
in that room with the eight Vicissitudes,
six Stages of Metta, four Noble Truths,
three Kinds of Suffering and two
ceiling fans spinning, spinning. She was
sitting on the other side of the room,
touching herself. I couldn't help staring.
She was twisting a strand of her long hair
round her fingers absent-mindedly,
listening to the speaker, holding it up
to her lips, sniffing it, tasting it,
eyeing it doubtfully, then letting it go.
She caressed her cheek, her forehead,
the palm of her hand cupped her chin, fingers
drumming. It was a pensive attitude
lasting only a moment, for her hands
grew restless again, and she started hugging
herself, her left hand massaging her right
shoulder, her right hand making excursions
to the hip, belly, armpit where it moored itself
with a thumb camped out on the small hillock
of her left breast. I couldn't help wondering
if she could feel my eyes on her body the way I could
feel her hands on her body on mine. "Don't
attach to anything as *me* or *mine*," the Buddhist
speaker who was Jewish before he was Buddhist
was saying, "because attachment is the second
arrow." That's when I realized I had missed
what the first arrow was. And then, as in a dream,
I was trying to raise one of my hands lying
in my lap like two dead birds, belly-up, to ask.

THE CONVERSATIONS OF MEN

My girlfriend says she would like to be a fly
on the wall between two urinals.
What would she overhear? she asks me.
I tell her the last time a man spoke to me
above a urinal, I think he said, "How about them Bruins?"
And what did I say in return? she wants to know.
I say I didn't know what to say because
I don't know anything about hockey,
and I didn't watch the game or even know
there was one. But I didn't want him
to know that. So I think I said, "Goddamn!"
because it sounded heartfelt yet noncommittal,
because he may or may not have been a Bruins fan,
and because the Bruins may or may not have won,
and because he was trying to make contact
with his gender, and if I said I didn't see the game,
or if I said I didn't follow hockey or don't
give a shit about the Bruins, he would probably
feel like he hadn't made contact. And I would feel
less of a man. So I said, "Goddamn!" and he said
"Unbelievable!" and shook his head in approval,
or maybe it was disapproval—it was hard to tell, I tell her,
because the whole thing was more or less peripheral.

Paul Hostovsky

CHOLERA

In the dream you said, "I love
this time of day—it's called the cholera."
I said I thought the cholera was a disease.
You said, "It *is* a disease but it's also
a time of day." There was no dictionary
in the dream, and we were sitting outside
at a café or a hospital. You asked if I'd read
Love in the Time of Cholera, and I said
I started it once, but never got past the first
50 pages. And you said, "That explains it."
I wondered if you meant the book explains
the time of day you love and why it's called
the cholera; or if you meant something else,
something about me and the way I am, namely,
someone who can't get past the first 50 pages
of a book you love. Which would mean
something else entirely. And then I said
"I think cholera is one of those words that,
if divorced from its meaning, would make a beautiful
name for a girl. Like Treblinka." You gave me
a pained look in the dream then, and I wondered
if it meant you didn't agree with me, or if it meant
that what you were eating didn't agree with you.
Either way, it was plain to see you were suffering.

DINOSAURS

The children love the dinosaurs because
the dinosaurs were doomed too
and didn't know it either. Take, for example,
this group of fourth graders
pushing and shoving and shuffling through the Museum
of Natural History, like a long line of
cockeyed cursive letters in a penmanship book,
each resting a hand on the shoulder of the next,
walking elephant-fashion under the enormous
skeletons, whose names are so long that
if you stood them up vertically
they might reach the small brains
of the dinosaurs themselves. Poor little
mammoths, disappearing off the face of
themselves, growing up much too soon—
already they are beginning to forget
what the rest of us can't for the life of us
remember either. First their imaginations
will dry up, then they'll spend their lives
putting out volcanoes, and eating their rivals,
and straining upward with pursed, prehensile lips
toward happiness, that greenest, furthest frond in the canopy.

Paul Hostovsky

DECLINE

Alone on top I'd take out my harmonica
and send a few notes bending down the valley.
Whatever I gave the valley the valley would echo,
rendering it exactly, only more lovely.
Liking the thought of that, I'd try the same
with several lines of mediocre verse;
or, certain I was alone, with my own name,
then my own name followed by my applause.

But always inevitably this deteriorated
into a stream of consciousness string of profanities
which didn't bear repeating, but which always
the singing valley nevertheless repeated.
That none was disturbed by this, not even the trees,
was better than song or poem, sweeter than praise.

POETRY AT THE BURGER KING

Where is it? It's not here.
All these plastic chairs and tables
are empty. Nothing but a lot of
dead meat here, and this associate
behind the counter mumbling: *Welcome
to Burger King, may I take your order?*
Mine is the only car outside in the sad
parking lot ringed by a handful
of gimpy trees, a blue dumpster in the corner.
Beyond that, the highway where I
came from, and where I will return.
If your daily life seems poor, said Rainer
Maria Rilke, do not blame *it.* Blame yourself.
Tell yourself you are not poet enough
to call forth its riches. I'm fingering a salty
corner of my empty French fries pocket,
licking my fingers, looking out the window
and telling myself I am not poet enough,
when I notice two kids running, sort of
galloping, sort of hopscotching across
the sad parking lot ahead of their parents
and into the Burger King. They are
very happy to be here, this little girl and boy,
jumping up and down now at the counter,
dancing to the song of the associate
which wasn't a song until their dancing
made it so. There are so many riches
on the menu, they can't make up their minds.
And while their parents order they play
duck duck goose, touching all the tables,
and all the chairs, the girl behind the boy,
following him, copying him and laughing
louder and louder, because it's all so wonderful

Paul Hostovsky

here at the Burger King, which they seem to have
all to themselves, except for one man in a booth
smiling, writing something down on a piece of paper.

GATES OF LOVE

He isn't old enough
to be sitting up front
but I let him,
my little interlocutor
asking me if they had cars
back when I was growing up—
and something clicks
into place
behind my ears
as my own smile
lifts like a drawbridge
with a clockwork
deep inside my chest,
and a sloop with me in it
waving to myself
passes steeply underneath,
his seatbelt riding up against
his cheek, his little mug
holding the question up
to my right ear,
the road to school unfolding
like an old familiar story
with a horse and carriage in it
and two riders
with hats. . .

Once upon a time
in the 1960s
they had cars, but the cars
didn't have seatbelts,
so when they braked
the long right arms of the mothers
automatically extended themselves

Paul Hostovsky

across the chests
of the children riding up front—
those maternal
turnstiles, those gates of love
coming down in the front seats
of cars braking
all across America,
that pressure at chest level, that feeling
loved, protected, held
up in the front seat
of America
can still be felt
by those of us who are old enough
to remember,
and maybe by extension
by those of us who aren't.

BOY WITH FATHER WITH FOREIGN ACCENT

My father's name is Egon,
pronounced *egg* on.
He grew up in Czechoslovakia
so he pronounces a lot of his words

wrong. I help him with that and in turn
he helps me spell Czechoslovakia.
I'm the only kid in my class who can.
I'm writing it now on the placemat

at the International House of Pancakes.
We're international, me and Egon,
sitting across from each other in our booth
like nations at the table. A language

is a dialect with an army, so I drill him
in the names of all the syrups, and he
drills me in C-z-e-c-h-o-s-l-o-v-a-k-i-a
while we wait for my pancakes and his eggs.

"Egg on your face," I say to him,
and he reaches for a napkin.
"It's just an expression," I explain,
and he asks me what it means. I say

I'm not sure, but whenever I hear it
it makes me think of him. "You have Egon
on your face," he says. And I patiently
correct him. But he says again, "You have

Egon on your face—you have my nose
and mouth and chin. Egon on your face—
and you can't wipe him off."

Paul Hostovsky

O WORLD I CANNOT HOLD THEE CLOSE ENOUGH

Sometimes I question the whole
Enterprise, I mean the whole
Thing, the whole
Universe, which is the one
Verse, the one great
Poem. Sometimes I think
it sucks so bad it's beyond
revision, beyond
hope. I mean after the Big
Bang, I mean after the First
Fuck, they should have just
flushed it down a black hole,
you know? I mean it would have
saved us all a lot of Time and
Space. But I only
think that sometimes. Other times
I want to open a window
and make love to the whole
World, I mean the whole
Earth. Sometimes I want
to sniff Earth's crotch so bad I can taste it.
This usually happens in the spring
when the sweet and sour morning breath
of Earth just waking up, the sweaty
neck and breasts and tangled hair
and ripe armpits of Earth
stretching after long sleep
can make me fall in love with the whole
World, the whole
Enterprise of Earth, and all I want
is to lick the sleep from Earth's eyes,
lick the milk from Earth's magnificent nipples,

smell the faintly sweet irresistible smell
of urine on Earth's sheets,
and just follow it to its source,
sniffing it out, licking it, eating it, loving it.

FRISBEE

We are all attracted to suffering.
And repulsed by it, too.
This doesn't make the world go round exactly.
It isn't a law of physics, technically.
But it may have something to do
with the relationships of bodies
in the universe. And also the atmosphere
of Earth. Which is where we all must live
for as long as we have left. For as long as we have
lift. And when you consider all of the plastic
found in the stomachs of dead seabirds—
bits of beach toy, medical waste, gnarled
cassette tape, whole flash drives, a red-striped
straw—it kind of makes you feel ashamed
of your own life. The way a seagull
rides the wind, oscillating, is almost as old
as the wind itself. What's new is
the adult birds can't tell the difference
between food and plastic, and they end up
feeding it to their young. It's a wonder
they can fly at all. In particle physics
there are six different kinds of quarks
known as flavors: up, down, charm, strange, top
and bottom. We used to smoke a lot of marijuana,
then practice throwing and catching them until dark:
forehand, backhand, overhead, under
the legs, behind the back and upside-down.
When my stomach hurts I go lie down
and try to think about something else.
But my thoughts always come back to the pain
as though it were a kind of home.

NAUGHTON'S QUARTERS

Sometimes when I'm walking
in the cemetery
I steal a few
quarters from Naughton

because I need them
for the parking meters
when I'm driving.
This I confide to a friend

over lunch, adding:
Naughton has plenty
and doesn't drive anymore anyway,
and it's not like Naughton's neighbors

notice. Plus his descendents
keep replenishing them—
it must be some kind of tradition,
like placing stones, or flowers—

and then there's the tradition
I'm upholding: the grave-
robber's tradition, the living taking from the dead
what the dead have no need of.

My friend stops chewing.
He looks alarmed, pillaged,
like he just bit down on something hard
and realized it was his own filling.

Put the quarters back, he says.
The dead have need. They have need.

Paul Hostovsky

TEMPLE

The peace of God
is a piece of cake.
Heaven is here.
Heaven is now.
God's temple
is a relationship.
It's any relationship.
It's every relationship.
Take a look
around. The world is full of
temples. Join one.
Join them all.
Join. Join. Join.
Joy. Joy. Joy.
The joy of God
is a piece of joinery.
It's a joint.

THE WAY OUT

The way out
isn't under or
over or around
or even through.
It's with. With is
the only way out.
In fact, out isn't
the way out either.
Out is a misnomer.

IV. LETTING GO

MIRACLES

Spiritual texts are the most boring books in the world.
None of them mentions a bicycle
or a Ferris wheel, or baseball, or sea lions, or ice cream.
They just lump them all together into "the world."
The "world of appearances." The "world of illusions."
You can walk through this world and not
believe it for a minute. You can get to the end of it
and not believe that either. The miracle is seeing
right through the world to another
world that's right here, right now.
But you have to let go of everything.
You have to let go of everything—you can
start by letting go of these words, just let them
go. Let them fall through the air, skim
your knee, spill to the floor. How to read these words
when they're lying on the floor face-down
like bodies? That is the seeming difficulty.
You can sit in a small room all alone with your body
and not believe it for a minute. You can
don the humble johnny that closes in the back,
and when the doctor comes in with his numbers
which are your numbers, you can
not believe that either. You can let them fall from his lips,
skim your ear, pool on the floor where your eyes
and his eyes have fallen. He won't
mention the bicycle, or the Ferris wheel which is
taking up a lot of room right now in the little
examining room where a sea lion has clambered up
onto the table and is barking, and the baseballs are flying,
and the vendors are hawking ice cream—because he can't
see them. He can't perform a miracle.

TREE POEM

It wasn't that he wanted to take his life.
He wanted to take his death
into his own hands. There was
a difference, he knew, though he couldn't
articulate it. More speculative than suicidal,
more curious than depressed,
more interested than not,
he didn't want to talk to a therapist.
He wanted to talk to Walt Whitman.
He wanted to talk to his best friend from
kindergarten, who'd moved away
on the cusp of first grade, and he never
saw him again. He wanted to climb a tree
and sit up there all alone in the top branches
watching it absorb the carbon dioxide.
He had a bit of the tree in him himself.
He had similar aspirations
and spent much of his time in the branching
ramifications in his head. But because his children
would never live it down, he climbed
down from the tree in the car in the garage
every time, and walked back into his life with a few
leaves and twigs still sticking to his head.

Paul Hostovsky

HOLY INSTANT

The way she
looked out the window,
sitting on the edge of the bed,

doing those little
exercises with her feet,
the physical therapist kneeling

on the hospital floor in front of her,
teaching her how, praising her—
the way she

looked out the window then,
not at the trees, or the buildings, or the sky—
not *at* anything,

just out. Just away.
The way she looked away
when the therapist praised her, saying:
"That's very good, Marguerite."

SURVIVOR

The first time we kissed
you turned away, saying:
"Not on the mouth. Not yet. I'm
sorry. There are things
I haven't told you."
I didn't understand.
But I understood enough
to gather your hands
in my hands,
to rest my cheek
against yours,
then to kiss
your cheek,
your temple, your
eyebrow,
and then only
the side
of your mouth,
its corner. It was
a sort of lateral kiss,
like looking a little to one side
of a thing to see it better,
like with stars,
or with poems,
or like the truck that carries the glass
on its side,
because of the nature of its cargo.

Paul Hostovsky

POEM FOR MICHAEL JACKSON

I can't stop thinking about you, Michael Jackson,
brother, son, father, sun, burn victim, king.
You were richer than God, and lonelier.
We had a lot in common, you and I. We were
both born in 1958, and around the time
of your death I was contemplating my own
euthanasia, having gotten the cancer diagnosis
a few months before. I wear a white cotton glove
to bed when my hand eczema acts up. I have done
the moonwalk, or tried, in my socks on my kitchen floor.
I have looked at children and found them beautiful,
not sexy beautiful or movie-star beautiful,
but I've-loved-you-ever-since-you-were-born-and-probably-
        longer-than-that
beautiful; and have wanted, needed, to be near them.
Your music was playing on the radio in radiation
oncology, and the nurses were talking about you behind
my back as I lay face-down on the table, my butt
hanging out, waiting for them to line up the machine
and zap me with the healing poison. It felt a lot like
your life, I imagined, the sublime rhythm of the music
competing for air with all the sniggering, gossiping,
excoriating voices buzzing around your head. The nurses
said the cruelest things about you while you were singing
about love in a child's voice, just one day after your death.
And I wanted to say something to them, something
in defense of you, something in praise of you, something
in memoriam. So I jumped up off the table with my
johnny flapping around in the dead air of that dead
room full of news of your death, and my death, and I
moonwalked as best I could with my family jewels flopping
up and down in front of their dropped jaws and popping

pathological eyes, right out the door of radiation oncology,
    singing
with you, dancing with you, standing with you, Michael Jackson.

Paul Hostovsky

TURNING FIFTY

It was a beautiful day, rainy-gray, foggy, dismal, perfect.
I was so happy because there was nothing to do
and nowhere to go and no one to meet and never
in my life had I felt so empty and so full. I wanted to sneeze
or to cum. I wanted to die. I wanted a drink
though I hadn't had a drink in seventeen years.
But I didn't really want a drink, I just wanted
to climb a tree that no longer stood where it stood
and hide up there all alone in the top branches
and look down at a world that no longer looked
like it looked. Do you know what I mean? I mean the smell
of the rain before the rain and after the rain
as opposed to the rain itself. I walked up and down
the wet streets, looking at all of the houses
that I would never set foot in. So easy to love them,
the shapes of those lives, their windows like the dark
eyes of beautiful young girls, who are too young
and too beautiful, forbidden and far-away and impossible as
life on Mars, all of the newspapers of Earth clamoring: *Life on Mars!*

WAITING ROOM

The woman with the portable oxygen tank
is standing in front of the exotic fish tank
looking at the fish. The woman looks like the fish
with her bulging eyes and yellow raincoat and exotic
portable oxygen tank. The fish tank is
too small for the fish, thinks the woman. If only
it were bigger, she could breathe easier.
The fish swim back and forth, back and forth,
looking for the way out. They think there is one.
They think if they keep looking they will find it.
Death is the only way out of the exotic fish tank,
thinks the woman. The dead ones are lifted out
by a living hand, which the fish probably think
is the long hand of Death. It scares them and they
scatter. But it's the same hand that feeds them,
this hand that lifts them gently up when they are
no more. It cares for them. It loves them. It would
hold them to itself, if only they could be held and
live. But they can't, thinks the woman, looking down
at the small bones of her own hand, and lifting it up
to adjust her breathing tube, inhales jaggedly, floats away.

THE ANGER OF ANNE FRANK

You can hide a concentration camp just about anywhere.
There, for example, behind those trees.
There's a little opening just around the corner—
you can't quite see it from here—
where the cement trucks keep coming and going.
What on earth are they building in there anyway?
But to hide a Jew, one Jew,
not to mention a family of Jews, two families,
two families and one lovesick dentist—
Jewish of course—
and then on top of that, or somehow inside of it,
to hide an anger as loud as a city,
yet more powerless than a petty official
in a very small town
where everyone's practically related—
War is one thing, but a dentist
who shuts himself up in a bathroom for hours—
what on earth is he building in there anyway?
You can hide what you do, you can hide what you think,
but try and hide a feeling, one feeling,
not to mention all the feelings that could fill a book.
You could fill a book, you could hide that book,
but to hide one stomachache, one heartache, one heart's
bad weather—not to mention all the good and beautiful weather—
well that is something some do better than others.
Mothers hide it better than daughters.

SMALL THING

"And this is Uli Detling—
she had a lisp," says Aunt Edie
who has dementia,
but can still remember Uli
Detling and her lisp
from 60 years ago,
but cannot remember
having already said this to me
just two minutes ago,
as we page through my mother's
wedding album together.
She says again, "And here
is Uli Detling, a friend of the family—
she had a lisp." And here is Edie.
And here is Edie in her light blue
taffeta dress—she can't be more than
16—at my parents' wedding, standing
beside my mother, grinning. And here
I wasn't even born yet. I think
I can remember back to when I was 4,
or maybe 3. But before that
I can't remember. I can't remember my first
attempts at forming words, or the taste
of my mother's milk, or being
born. And I can't remember
not being. And I can't remember
God. Sometimes I have glimpses though—
moments when I can sort of remember
something of God. Not all of God, but
some small thing. "And this
is Uncle Herman. And this is
Aunt Miriam. And I think this is
Uli Detling, yes, she was a friend
of the family. Poor thing, she had a lisp."

Paul Hostovsky

FRAME

If you framed some photos of people you don't know
and put them up on your mantelpiece and piano,
on your desk and dresser and end tables,
or just hung them on all the walls—you'd be surrounded
by pictures of smiling people you would probably
never meet in your life, faces of total strangers
who nevertheless, over time, would begin to grow
familiar to you, intimate even, strangely, namelessly
known. And if someday, somewhere, somehow
you began to run into them out in the world,
wouldn't it feel like coming home? Wouldn't it feel
like love, the kind of love you only feel for your own
children, whom you love so much it hurts, even now
that they're grown, distant, reticent, strangers almost?

IN PRAISE OF THE QUITTER

Praise the quitter for standing up
for something more important than not giving up,
something more worth fighting for than
simply winning, or simply living, namely,
seeing—that there is another way,
a quiet, leaf-strewn way that leads
off the battlefield and down through the trees
to somewhere you can't see from here,
though he sees it, the way others see
victory, and they stand up for the team,
and they step up to the plate—he stands and steps
lightly off the field and into the adjacent
woods, walking softly down a path
where the courtships of small animals go on
in the leaves, and the birds are tunneling
and darting up through the ramifications
to the top branches, the best seats, where they look
out over the fields of life. And what they see is
not the games, not the people playing the games;
what they see is what the quitter sees: a great sky
and earth, and lots of little bugs swimming around
for their dear short lives, which are shorter
than an inning; half an inning; shorter than a swing.
Praise the quitter flapping his tiny insect-wings—
he is aerodynamically impossible, yet look at him
go! swimming against the rules, flying against
the odds, up through the air and off into the sunset.

Paul Hostovsky

THE GOOD NEWS

The good news is
you're wrong.
About everything.
The bad news is
not what you thought.
The good news is
not what you thought.
That's the good news.
And it's greater
than you know.
And it's greater
than you can imagine—
you can't imagine
being wrong about
everything. That's why
the good news is
so unimaginable.
For starters, you're wrong
about who you are—
about *what* you are,
and where you are,
and what you are doing,
and what you think is being
done to you. I don't
know about you but
for some of us
that's very good news.
I'm not what I thought.
You're not what I thought.
You're not what you thought
either. And neither is
your mother. You needn't
figure it out. You needn't

bother. You need do nothing
but plead ignorance
at every turn,
and keep returning,
keep opening
to the great
good news.

OF COURSE

I think the dying say of course
just before they die, as though
they saw something that explained
everything. I think the Bible says
no one can see the face of God and live.
I think if you have never seen
the face of God, then you have never lived.
I think the dying say of course because
they see the face of God was right there,
right in front of their faces, right
under their noses, all the time, all the time.
And all the time they spent looking for it
or not looking for it, thinking about it or
never giving it a thought, it was right
there like a thought itself, on the tip
of morning, the tip of waking. Of course
we are asleep. Of course we will wake.
And when we do we will say of course
the way we say it all the time now, in our sleep.

SPLINTER

Because he felt nothing,
because he felt he couldn't
feel, he felt he couldn't
love, and he lifted
the wooden door of the garage
which housed the car which
housed the easeful death
which he was half in love with,
when a small dark
insidious grace
entered his left palm
near the thumb
and lodged itself there
and he winced in pain,
and let go of his plan,
holding the injured hand
in the uninjured one,
holding it up to his mouth
as though drinking from it,
or eating from it,
or weeping into it,
and in this attitude walked
back into his life.

Paul Hostovsky

UPLIFTING POEM

Look, this poem
can't hold you up.
It's holding itself up
as proof of its own
weakness. Look
how thin it is, how
frail, how feverishly
it mutters to itself
lurching down the
sidewalk of the
page. This is not
an uplifting poem
though once a long
time ago it was.
Once upon a time
there was a live chicken
in this poem,
there was a glacier
and a sailboat,
the Pacific Ocean
sloshing between stanzas,
and you like Adam
saying *Here am I*
to God who was also
near. But now it's
close to the end.
Now there is no
lift left. You're
disappointed. Look,
the poem isn't sorry
you didn't find
what you came here for.
The poem isn't sorry

it didn't change
its name when its body
and its bearing changed.
The poem isn't a sorry poem.
It's much too proud
and a little too late
for that now.

THE CUP

When I find it in the basement
on the shelf above the dryer
under a pile of his old undershirts

I take it down and turn it over
and over, remembering how
uncomfortable he said it was

in spite of the rubber edge
and vent-holes, the plastic shell
shaped to fit a twelve-year-old penis

and testicles, which were being
tested on the football field that first
day at Pop Warner. All the fathers

stood around, talking football,
but all I could contribute was,
"Growing up, I played soccer myself..."

Then I was standing a little apart
like a pedestrian looking for my son
in traffic—football helmets and identical

red jerseys in gridlock, and I couldn't
find him. Because I couldn't remember
his number, and they all looked the same

running around out there for the love of
yardage. I felt a little panicky. Technically,
I'd lost him, lost sight of him, and everyone

knows what happens to kids who fall through
the hatches on the football fields of life...
Then I noticed—hanging back in the end zone

all alone—number 26, adjusting his protective
cup. And I kept my eyes on him until
the day he left for college. And finding it now

all these years later, I hold it for a moment
against my own testicles, whence he came. And then
I hold it up to my face, like an oxygen mask.

　　　　　　　　　　　　　　　　　Paul Hostovsky